CCSS Genre Exposito

MW00513176

Essential Question
How do people respond to natural disasters?

CHANGING LANDSCAPES
— BY MARIA GILL —

INTRODUCTION

Imagine you step into a time machine and travel thousands of years back in time. You step out and notice a landscape that looks very different from the one you left. There are high mountains instead of hills. The river cuts straight through the land instead of meandering. And where did those towering cliffs come from?

The time machine didn't make a mistake. This *is* what the place where you live looked like thousands of years ago. Why does it look so different?

Water carved out this canyon.

A hurricane causes huge waves, which can quickly reshape the coastline.

Earth's surface is always changing. Some of the biggest changes are those that happen gradually over thousands of years. Mountains slowly wear away, rivers create valleys and plains, and the ocean shapes the coast. Most of these changes happen too slowly for people to even notice.

However, people do notice natural disasters, such as hurricanes, floods, or landslides. Natural disasters alter the landscape suddenly and often cause severe damage. The impact of natural disasters can be less extreme in some places than in others. This is because some landscapes have natural features that help to protect the land.

CHAPTER 1

CRUMBLING LANDSCAPES

You might not think a trickle of water has much power, but over time, it creates big changes. Water changes and shapes Earth's surface in many ways.

In the mountains, rain collects in rivers and streams. As rivers flow downhill, rocks, sand, and **silt** are swept along. This mixture is called sediment. The water in fast-moving rivers can pick up and carry large rocks.

When the river or stream reaches flatter land, it deposits, or leaves behind, some of the sediment it is carrying. The movement of rocks, sand, and silt is called **erosion**.

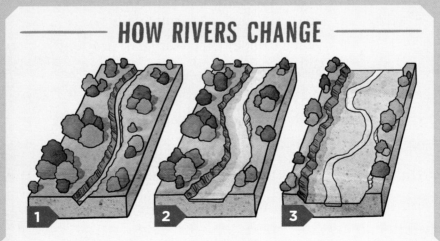

HOW RIVERS CHANGE

1. A fast-moving river cuts a path through the land.
2. Over time, the river wears away more of the land. The river widens.
3. The river deposits sediment and forms a plain.

Erosion has worn away these cliffs and created rock formations called sea stacks.

Water also changes how coastal areas look. Waves can wash away some areas of the coast and build up others.

Waves form when wind blows over the surface of the ocean. Waves have the power to break apart giant boulders. As they crash against a rock face, waves force water and air into cracks. Over time, these cracks expand and the rock splits.

Waves can wear away the bottom of cliffs. As waves swirl around the bases of cliffs, they wear down the rock, turning it into sand and silt. When larger rocks are broken down into smaller pieces, it is called **weathering**.

Wind also causes erosion. Wind, like water, lifts and moves sand around. The wind blows the sand, and hills of sand called dunes form.

5

Erosion is always happening, but some **environments** have natural features that slow it down. On beaches, wind blowing in from the ocean piles up sand to form sand dunes. Plants quickly grow on the dunes, trapping even more sand. Over time, dunes can grow very high. Large dunes act as **barriers**, sheltering inland areas from wind and wave erosion.

Wetlands also slow down erosion. Also known as marshes or swamps, wetlands are areas of land that are usually covered in shallow water that can be salty or fresh. Wetlands are found near the edges of rivers and lakes. They also form along the coastline and in places where rivers and streams empty into the ocean.

Wetlands act like nature's sponges. By absorbing and storing rainwater, they help to prevent flooding. During periods without rain, they release water and feed streams and rivers.

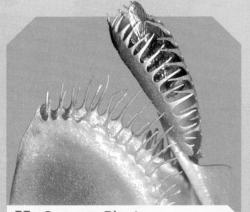

Steven P. Lynch

>> Swamp Plants

The Venus flytrap is one of the unusual plants that live in wetland areas. It has adapted to living in soil that has few nutrients. Instead, it gets nutrients from feeding on insects. The Venus flytrap uses its bright color and sweet nectar to lure insects.

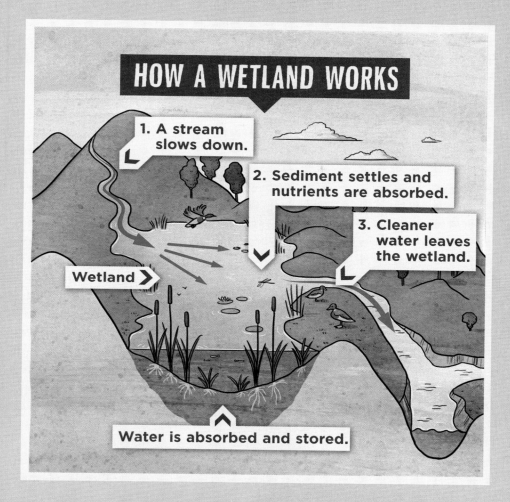

HOW A WETLAND WORKS

1. A stream slows down.

2. Sediment settles and nutrients are absorbed.

3. Cleaner water leaves the wetland.

Wetland

Water is absorbed and stored.

Water from streams and rivers slows as it flows through a wetland. This allows any sediment in the water to settle in the wetland.

Some plants have adapted to the wetland habitat and are able to grow in shallow water. These plants hold the soil in place. They absorb nutrients and help to purify or clean the water. In this way, wetlands act like filters, as well as sponges.

CHAPTER 2

SUDDEN CHANGES!

La Conchita, in California, was badly damaged by a landslide when a massive chunk of earth slid down the hillside onto the houses and buildings below.

Erosion usually changes the shape of Earth very slowly. However, natural disasters speed up erosion and can cause sudden changes.

Heavy rainfall and sometimes melting snow can trigger landslides. The ground becomes so waterlogged it can't absorb any more water and the land gives way. Rocks and soil begin to slide downhill faster and faster. If enough rocks and soil tumble down, a whole hillside can collapse. Landslides change the landscape by moving a lot of soil and rock all at once.

Landslides are also caused by unpredictable events such as earthquakes or volcanic eruptions. These natural forces can loosen and move weathered rocks and soil, sending them down hillsides.

Landslides can move with the speed and power of an express train, making them very dangerous. Huge amounts of rocks and soil can slide down a hillside in minutes. Landslides can cause millions of dollars of damage to roads, bridges, and buildings.

Landslides often happen in hilly areas where there are no trees and few plants. Trees and plants spread their roots deep underground. Their roots help to keep the soil in place. Trees and plants also absorb water in the soil.

The wind and water from hurricanes also cause sudden changes to the landscape. Hurricanes can be up to 500 miles wide and have wind speeds of up to 150 miles (240 km) an hour.

These violent storms form far out in the ocean. As a hurricane nears land, the wind can create substantial waves more than 40 feet high. The waves cause a lot of destruction when they reach land. These waves smash through storm barriers and remove sand from beaches. After a hurricane, a beach can be much smaller.

The high winds and the flood waters from Hurricane Katrina caused widespread damage in New Orleans.

Hurricanes bring heavy rainfall as well as high winds. This often leads to substantial flooding. Rivers can overflow their banks. Sand and sediment from the river are deposited on the land.

Coastal wetlands help to protect inland areas from hurricanes. When a hurricane hits the shore, the waves surge like a wall of water. Wetlands absorb and slow down some of that water. Hurricanes also weaken as they move across land. So coastal wetlands act as a buffer between the ocean and inland areas.

›› Hurricane Katrina

In 2005, Hurricane Katrina was a crisis for people living along the Gulf Coast. When the hurricane hit, a two-story-tall wall of water tore through levees and riverbanks in more than 50 places and flooded low-lying areas. Thousands of people were killed or made homeless.

When we take away natural features such as sand dunes and wetlands, more erosion can occur. Wetlands and dunes can disappear as towns and cities grow. Wetland areas have also been filled so farmers can grow crops or graze animals. Scientists estimate that approximately half of the wetland areas in the United States have been destroyed. This has caused more erosion and has increased the risk of flooding.

Areas where trees and plants have been cut down are also in danger. If the roots of trees and plants are no longer there, rain runs off these surfaces, causing erosion or even landslides.

To help slow down erosion and prevent landslides, we can plant trees and plants that have long, deep roots. This makes the land more stable.

Trees and plants with deep roots help stabilize the land.

(l) watershed regeneration by AMURT Haiti. © Subuddhyananda, (r) An example of the results of watershed regeneration © Subuddhyananda

These days, people realize that wetlands and dunes help to reduce erosion and flooding. Although people have built on many wetland areas, there are people who are working to **restore** these natural sponges.

We now know that wetlands are as important to the land as kidneys are to the human body. They control the flow of water and keep it clean.

Research is an important part of restoration. Before you can repair any environmental damage, you need to know what's causing it. Then you can make plans and take action, such as planting grasses in wetlands or rebuilding sand dunes.

Restoring wetlands helps prevent erosion.

CONLUSION

Imagine we could step back into our time machine and stop every 100,000 years. We would see the changes to mountains, rivers, and coasts that are caused by weathering and erosion. These changes happen very slowly.

Natural disasters such as hurricanes and landslides can cause sudden and destructive changes. We can't prevent natural disasters, but by restoring nature's barriers and sponges, such as wetlands and dunes, we can lessen the effects of erosion and make our environments more **resilient**.

Students plant grasses at a wetland area in Maryland.

Respond to Reading

Summarize

Use details from *Changing Landscapes* to summarize the selection. Your graphic organizer may help you.

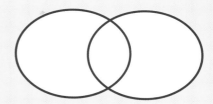

Text Evidence

1. How can you tell that *Changing Landscapes* is an expository text? GENRE

2. Reread pages 6 and 7. Compare and contrast how sand dunes and wetlands prevent erosion. COMPARE AND CONTRAST

3. What is the meaning of *shapes* on page 4? Use context clues to help you figure out the correct meaning. MULTIPLE-MEANING WORDS

4. Write about the similarities and differences between landslides and hurricanes. Use details from the text in your answer. WRITE ABOUT READING

Compare Texts

Read about how students in Florida are helping to prevent erosion.

Students Save Wetlands

Over the past 100 years, many wetland areas in Tampa Bay, Florida, have been destroyed to build houses, roads, and stores. Many wetland plants are gone, and fish and shellfish numbers have dropped.

Today people know that wetlands can prevent erosion, buffer the area against storms, and improve the quality of the water.

Students in the Tampa Bay area are working to restore the area's wetlands. They are growing and planting wetland grasses. They are also learning about the environment of Tampa Bay.

How to Grow Wetland Grasses

1. The students plant grasses in the school's nursery pond.

2. They check the growth of the grasses and test the water. The water needs to have the right amount of salt in it.

3. After six to eight months, the students dig up and separate the grasses. They replant half of their grasses so they have more room to grow.

4. Finally, once the grasses in the nursery pond have grown enough, the students replant them in a wetland area in Tampa Bay.

Healthy Coastal Areas

The grasses the students have planted will help provide stability for the shoreline and prevent erosion.

The grasses will also provide important habitats for the animals, birds, and fish living there. There are around 200 species of fish in the Bay. Thousands of birds nest in the area each year.

The students are proud to help in the Bay's restoration. They have made a big difference. In one year, they were able to restore almost 24 acres of wetland along the Florida coast.

The restoration of wetlands provides homes for birds such as the white ibis.

Make Connections

Why is restoring coastal areas important?

ESSENTIAL QUESTION

How do people in *Changing Landscapes* and *Students Save Wetlands* prevent erosion?

TEXT TO TEXT

Glossary

barriers *(BAR-ee-urz)* obstacles that stop things from getting through *(page 6)*

environments *(in-VIGH-ruhn-muhnts)* the places where animals or plants live *(page 6)*

erosion *(i-ROH-zhuhn)* the movement of rock caused by rain, wind, or glacial ice *(page 4)*

resilient *(ri-ZIL-yuhnt)* strong, able to recover quickly *(page 14)*

restore *(ri-STAWR)* return something to how it was *(page 13)*

silt *(silt) small* particles, or pieces of sand, clay, or dirt *(page 4)*

weathering *(WETH-uhr-ing)* the slow wearing away of rocks *(page 5)*

wetlands *(WET-landz)* areas of land that are covered by shallow water for some parts of the year *(page 6)*

Index

Focus on Science

Purpose To understand the kinds of damage a natural disaster can cause and how to prepare in advance

Step 1 Pick a type of natural disaster you want to learn more about. You might choose a natural disaster that is common where you live.

Step 2 Using the library or the Internet, research the causes of the natural disaster and the kinds of damage that result from it.

Step 3 Research the ways that people can prepare in advance for the natural disaster, such as by buying canned food and bottled water, or by making an emergency kit.

Step 4 Create a poster that summarizes what you learned. Make sure you include what the disaster is, what causes the disaster to happen, the hazards it creates, and how people can prepare and stay safe.

Conclusion How are the ways someone can prepare for the disaster you researched similar to how someone can prepare for other disasters? How are they different?